Kitchen Primer: Dinner's Ready

Participant Handout

By
Laurie Zerga

For Chef-K®

Kitchen Primer: Dinner's Ready
Participant Handout

2018

For information regarding permissions, contact:

Laurie Zerga, founder
Chef-K
www.chef-k.com

Some portions of this course material have been obtained from public sources or by permission. The following is a list of sources from which this material has been drawn:

- Federal Drug Administration
- National Science Teachers Association (NSTA)
- United States Department of Agriculture (USDA)
- United States Department of Health and Human Services (HHS)

Course: Kitchen Primer: Dinner's Ready
Day 1

Day 1 overview

Description

You will learn basic kitchen safety and kitchen rules for the week. You will learn basic knife skills and then prepare a salad menu. This camp is regularly modified to reflect the latest USDA guidelines and recommendations. The Dinner's Ready camp follows the healthiest options using whole grains, flavoring with little salt, as well as no added sugar, and alternatives to butter with natural ingredients such as olive and coconut oil. Dessert throughout the camp is fresh seasonal fruit.

Objectives

1. Learn basic kitchen practices for the week for safety in the kitchen.
2. Review basic kitchen etiquette for Chef-K classes.
3. Learn basic knife skills.
4. Use knife skills to prepare vegetables for salad

Let's Make Salad Entrée Menu

Seasonal Vegetable Salad with Chicken

What will we do today?

- Review the week
- Review basic kitchen safety and kitchen etiquette
- Learn and practice knife skills
- Prepare and enjoy our menu

Camp Overview

This program focuses on simple familiar menus. You will learn to prepare traditional entrees that are tasty and nutritious. As always there is a focus on seasonal ingredients.

By the end of the week, you will have covered basic food preparation, reading recipes, cooking, and cleanup.

The class can accommodate up to 16 students. It provides you with tasting, tactile and hands on experience. Each day includes lesson handouts and recipes for your future reference.

Day/date	Mon	Tues	Wed	Thurs	Fri
Hour 0	Instructor setup	Instructor setup	Instructor setup	Instructor setup	Instructor setup
Hour 1	Intro and Knife Skills	Food Safety Sauté & Browning Technique	Sum of the Parts	Food Allergies What's in the Oven?	Celebration and certificates
Hour 2	Let's Make Salad Entrée Menu Prep Lunch	It's not just a Hamburger Menu Prep Lunch	Everyone likes Pasta Menu Prep Lunch	Basic Roasted Meal Menu Prep Lunch	Mexican Fiesta Menu Prep Lunch
Hour 3	Cleanup Day ends Instructor cleanup	Cleanup Day ends Instructor cleanup	Cleanup Day ends Instructor cleanup	Cleanup Day ends Instructor cleanup	Cleanup Day ends Instructor cleanup
	Menu	Menu	Menu	Menu	Menu
	Seasonal Vegetable Salad with Chicken	Salisbury steak with French Onion Sauce	Pasta with Red & Green Sauce	Oven Roasted Chicken	Turkey Tacos
	Fresh Fruit	Rice	Simple Salad	Roasted Potatoes & Vegetables	Guacamole & Salsa
		Sautéed Zucchini	Green Beans	Fresh Fruit	Calabacitas (vegetables)
		Fresh Fruit	Fresh Fruit		Fresh Fruit

Staying safe and healthy in the kitchen

Preparing for class

Your safety and health is very important. All participants must follow basic food handling safety procedures during all classes. In addition, you should be very careful when using all appliances, tools, and utensils in the kitchen. Be aware of your safety and the safety of those around you.

Before handling food: rules all participants must follow

- Wash your hands with hot, soapy water. Disposable wipes or hand sanitizer gel are not an alternative unless water is not available.
- Tie back long hair.
- Wear an apron if possible.
- Do not wear jackets.
- Do not wear extra long sleeves that can drag into food; all sleeves must be at least above wrists, and are better at ¾ lengths below elbow.
- Never eat, drink, or chew gum while preparing food. Keep your hands out of your mouth.
- Disinfect all surfaces with a disinfecting bleach solution or appropriate anti-bacterial cleaner.

Student safety

Student safety is important, so be sure to handle food properly.

About safe cleaning and safe disposing of waste

Washing Hands	Disinfecting	Sterilizing tools	Safely disposing of material
Use hot water. Wet hands and add soap. Scrub hands 20 seconds away from the running water. Rinse hands under running water. Dry hands with clean dry towels. Only if water is not available, use disposable wipes or hand sanitizer gel.	Make a bleach solution: 20 ml of bleach with 1 liter tap water. If bleach is not available, use antibacterial cleaner. Wipe counter of all visible soil. Spray all work surfaces and leave on for 2 minutes. Note: bleach solution loses effectiveness within 24 hours.	Wash all kitchen tools and utensils. If possible, use a dishwasher that has been tested for the correct temperature. If an appropriate dishwasher is not available, wash with hot soapy water and rinse.	Dispose of raw meat scraps by placing in a sturdy plastic bag. Seal and dispose of the bag. Recycle paper, glass jars, cans, and milk cartons. Place vegetable and fruit waste in the "green bin".

Using appliances, tools and utensils
- Be respectful of the heat. Stoves, pots and pans, as well as oil and water will get hot. Use appropriate oven mitts, hot pads, and trivets to protect yourself and counter tops.
- Knives and forks are sharp. Follow safety instructions to avoid cutting yourself or those near you.
- Electric appliances often have safety features, but participants should still be alert at all times when using them.

All participants must be respectful of their classmates during class. Inappropriate behavior will not be tolerated at any time in the kitchen.

Chef-K Kitchen Etiquette

During all activities, be respectful of the other participants, the instructors, and the assistants.

Inappropriate behavior is not tolerated at any time in the kitchen. Stoves are hot, and knives are sharp. Please help avoid injuring yourself or others.

Class starts on time; be considerate of others who arrive on time. No one may join more than 10 minutes after class starts. Our time is limited, and we need time to cook.

Come to class for the designated amount of time. Be courteous of other participants by not walking in and out of the room. If you have to leave, you are welcome to join us at the next class.

Do not bring any gum, drinks, or food into the room. Everyone will have an opportunity to share the meal that we prepare.

Before coming into the room, silence your cell phone.

When you arrive, remove your jacket, roll up long sleeves, and put long hair in a ponytail. If you are in a commercial kitchen, a hairnet or cap is required. Sign in and wash your hands.

Wear closed-toed shoes—not sandals or flip-flops.

Help clean as you go. If you do not have a specific food preparation task, look for something to clean up.

If you have not tasted something, please request a small taste. Food allergies are the only acceptable reason to avoid tasting. Be respectful if you do not like something that you taste.

When the meal is ready, please sit and enjoy the food that you have prepared.

If there are leftovers, you are welcome to take them home. The leftover food will be divided among the participants.

Knife Safety

A knife is one of the most important tools used in the kitchen. It is used to dice, julienne, mince, and slice food.

Important: Knives should be cared for properly and kept sharp. If not used carefully and with proper respect, they can cause serious injury.

Type of knife	Uses
Chef's knife	For preparing many kinds of ingredients. Usually the largest knife in the kitchen, a chef's knife has a wide blade that is 8 to 10 inches long. It is one of the most commonly used knives.
Paring knife	For peeling and coring fruits and vegetables, cutting small ingredients, and slicing. A paring knife's blade is 2½ to 4 inches long. It is one of the most commonly used knives.
Boning knife	For boning meat and trimming fat before cooking. A boning knife blade is 4 to 5 inches long and is flexible so that it can curve around meat and bone.
Bread knife	For slicing bread. A bread knife blade is 6 to 10 inches long and is serrated. When using a serrated knife, use a sawing motion. Most experts recommend a serrated knife that has pointed serrations, instead of wavy serrations, for better control and longer knife life.
Carving knife	For cutting cooked meat—for example, for carving a roast beef or a whole roasted chicken. A carving knife's blade is 10 to 12 inches long and is flexible to make it easier to cut off meat around bones.
Utility knife	For slicing meat and cheese. A utility knife is longer than a paring knife but smaller than a chef's knife. Its blade is 5 to 8 inches long. It is also called a sandwich knife.

Tips for Handling Knives Safely...use same edit notes from Brunch All Day

- Always pass a knife to another person with the handle toward the other person. The person taking the knife is presented with the handle rather than the blade or tip.

- Never run or cause a distraction while someone is using a knife in the same room.

- Keep knives clean and dry. A wet knife can slip out of your hand.

- Always keep knives sharp. Never use a knife's blade to scrape food off a cutting board because it dulls the knife. Never use a knife for anything but cutting food.

- Always use a cutting board to protect countertops. Consider putting damp paper towels or tacky shelf liner under the cutting board to prevent slippage.

- Always lay down knives with the blade flat. Do not put a knife down on the flat or sharp edge of the blade.

- *Never* try to catch a falling knife. Let the knife fall to the floor and then pick it up. It's safer to wear shoes while cooking so that a falling knife cannot cut your foot.

- Always wash a knife in warm, soapy water, with the blade away from you. Dry the knife and store it in a knife block or flat in a drawer. If you store a knife in a drawer, cover the blade with a knife guard, which is available at kitchen stores.

- Never leave a knife in a pan of soapy water. You could accidentally grab the knife by the blade and cut yourself.

- When walking through class with a knife, hold the knife beside your leg with the point down and call out, "knife coming through".

How to Hold a Knife

You will have an opportunity to try cutting different items throughout the week.

Always use your dominant (right or left) hand to hold a knife handle and use the other hand as a helper.

Note: For simplicity, the instructions and photographs in this procedure use a right-handed person as an example.

Claw and Dagger

1. Grasp the knife handle with your dominant (right or left) hand.

2. Curl the fingers of your other hand into a claw shape, and put your knuckles flat against the dull edge of the blade, keeping your fingers away from the sharp edge.

Figure 1: Holding a knife – claw and dagger

Note: For people with small hands, it is often easier to carefully hold the dull edge of the blade with the thumb and index finger while the other fingers grasp the knife's handle. This technique gives small hands more control over the knife.

Your helper hand—the "claw" hand—is at greatest risk of an accidental cut. However, when your hand is in a claw, your fingertips will not get cut.

Bridge

Sometimes, something you are cutting is too small to comfortably hold it with your claw. In this case you can use a bridge position for your helper hand.

1. Grasp the knife handle with your dominant (right or left) hand.

2. Place your thumb and pointer finger of your helper hand into an arch form. Then hold the food with thumb and finger. Take the knife and fit it between the arch or bridge of your hand and carefully, cut down the center of the food item.

Figure 2 – Holding a knife – bridge

Power Push – flat hand

Other times, when you are mincing herbs, or perhaps a food item is a bit hard to cut, you will need to put a bit of power into the knife. You can place your tip on the cutting board, start the cut and then place your helper hand on top of the knife with a flat hand. Use your body weight to push down.

Figure 3: Holding a knife – Power push

Cutting Fruits and Vegetables

If you are right-handed, hold the knife handle with your right hand and curl your left hand into a claw.

If you are left-handed, hold the knife handle with your left hand and curl your right hand into a claw. Put your "claw" hand on the food, with your fingers curled, and use your knuckles as a guide.

Figure 2: Curl your fingers and use your knuckles as a guide

Dicing, Chopping, or Mincing

Uncurl your "claw" hand and rest your fingers on the knife's dull edge.

Figure 3: Fingers on top (dull edge) of the knife

Knife Terminology

The recipes in this course use the following terms to refer to ways of cutting ingredients.

Term	What it means	Example
Chop	To cut into rough pieces. You can chop coarsely (into big pieces) or finely (into small pieces). Recipes often say *coarsely chop* or *finely chop*…	
Dice	To cut food into tiny (about $\frac{1}{8}$-inch to $\frac{1}{4}$-inch) cubes	
Julienne	To cut into very thin (matchstick-size) strips a. Cut the food into slices that are $\frac{1}{8}$ inch thick. b. Stack the slices and cut them into strips that are $\frac{1}{8}$ inch thick. c. Cut the strips to the desired length	
Mince	To chop into very small pieces (smaller than when chopped).	
Slice	To cut with a knife.	

Practice Using a Knife

Important: Carelessness or failure to follow the knife safety guidelines described in this class will result in a loss of the knife privileges. You will not be allowed to use a knife in class.

Practice holding a knife and cutting ingredients. After some practice, your instructor will confirm that you are doing it correctly. Once your instructor has confirmed that you can do the following knife tasks, you can use a knife in all Chef-K classes.

- Demonstrate how to hold a chef's knife.
- Julienne a carrot and a stalk of celery.
- Dice a carrot and a stalk of celery.
- Mince an herb.
- Peel and slice an onion.
- Demonstrate how to hold a paring knife.

Your instructor will log the results of your knife practice in the knife skills checklist.

Knife Safety Quiz

True/False

Directions: respond true or false to following questions:

1) When passing a knife to another person; always present the blade or tip to them.

2) Always make sure a knife is clean and dry before using it.

3) It's a good idea to use the blade to scrape food off of a cutting board.

4) It's best to leave a soiled knife in warm soapy water while you prepare the rest of your meal.

5) Always use a cutting board to protect your counter or table top.

6) If a knife falls it's best to try to catch it before it hits the ground.

7) For the purposes of our kitchen classes, if you are carrying a knife across the kitchen you should call out, "knife coming through."

Multiple choice – select the best answer from a to c

1) A good way to store a knife is:

    a. Laying flat in a drawer with a knife guard.

    b. In a knife block.

    c. Both a & b are good ways to store knives.

2) Always keep your knife sharp. The following helps to keep the knife sharp.

    a. Never scrape food off a cutting board with the blade.

    b. Never use a knife for anything except for cutting.

    c. All of the above.

Day 1: Let's Cook

Let's Make a Salad Entrée

Menu

Seasonal Vegetable Salad with Chicken
Fresh Fruit

Game plan

1. Prepare vegetable salad ingredients – reserve ends & scraps for poaching chicken
2. Poach chicken & let cool
3. Prepare the fruit
4. Assemble salad add sliced chicken and dress
5. Set the table and set out drinks.
6. Enjoy meal
7. Clear table.
8. Serve fresh fruit

Recipe: Simple Poached Chicken

Serves 8-10

Sometimes when you are preparing multiple recipes you have onion skins, pieces of extra carrots, or other vegetables. These are good to save and add to the poaching liquid to add flavor.

Ingredients

- 1-pound boneless, skinless chicken breast
- Vegetable ends and scraps (optional)
  Example: onion skin & root, ends of carrots
- Salt and pepper (1/8 tsp each or to taste)
- Water to cover

Directions

1. Place chicken breasts in a large pot
2. Add vegetable scraps if you are using them.
3. Season with salt and pepper
4. Add enough water to cover chicken by 1-inch
5. Bring to boil
6. Reduce heat and let simmer 20 minutes. Remove from heat and let cool to room temperature. Refrigerate until ready to slice for salad.

Recipe: Seasonal Vegetable Salad with Chicken

Serves 8

This is a wonderful salad created from whatever is in season. In early summer, you might find dainty bunches of carrots, new celery, tomatoes and early zucchini. Add an assortment of herbs and you'll have a wonderful crunchy salad. The chicken, cheese and toasted nuts mean it can be a meal in itself. Below finds an example of vegetables; but feel free to try others.

Ingredients

- 1 bunch of baby carrots diced (standard bulk carrots may be used if baby carrots are unavailable – about ½ pound)
- 2 zucchinis diced
- 2 ribs celery diced
- 1 basket of cherry tomatoes halved
- ¼ cup of pitted green olives
- ½ cup of shredded cheddar cheese of your choice
- ¼ cup of toasted pine nuts—or sunflower seeds or almonds
- 1pound poached boneless, skinless chicken breasts cut into slices
- Assorted fresh herbs, such as basil, thyme, parsley torn into pieces
- ¼ cup olive oil
- ¼ cup fresh lemon juice
- Salt & pepper to taste

Directions

1. Prepare all vegetables as described above. If the carrots are very tender and organic; it is not necessary to peel them. However, if they are standard carrots, have the participants peel them.
2. Combine vegetables, olives, cheese, nuts and herbs into a bowl
3. Gently toss with olive oil
4. Add lemon juice and salt and pepper.

Winter Option:

Eliminate zucchini, cherry tomatoes, green olives, and pine nuts
Use ¼ head of red cabbage sliced, 1 orange, peeled, and diced, and either sunflower seeds, or almonds.

Nutritional Values

Nutrient Name	Nutrient Value	Unit
Calories	290	
Total Fat	21	g
Saturated Fat	4	g
Trans Fat	0	g
Cholesterol	50	mg
Sodium	220	mg
Carbohydrates	7	g
Dietary Fiber	2	g
Sugars	3	g
Protein	20	g
Vitamin A		IU
Vitamin C		mg
Calcium		mg
Iron		mg

This dish qualifies for USDA low sodium dish.

Fresh Fruit

Serves 4

Ingredients

- ¼ pound fruit per person

Directions

1. Wash, dry, and slice fruit onto a platter for serving.

Sample fruit combinations:

- Assorted berries like strawberries, blueberries, raspberries, and blackberries.

- Melon, like cantaloupe, and honey dew

- Exotic fruit, like mango, pineapple, and bananas

- Stone fruit, like plums, nectarines, peaches, and apricots.

- Fall fruit, like apples, bananas, and pears.

- Winter fruit, like bananas, oranges, nectarines, and kiwi.

Nutrition varies by type of fruit.

Course: Kitchen Primer: Dinner's Ready
Day 2

Day 2 overview

Description
You will review food safety and the techniques of sautéing and browning.
You will then prepare a Salisbury steak menu.

Objectives
1. Learn food safety and build on kitchen practices from Day 1.
2. Practice basic knife safety and knife skills.
3. Understand the principle of sautéing and browning
4. Demonstrate the cooking with Salisbury steak with French onion sauce
5. Practice the techniques while preparing the menu for the day.

It's not just a Hamburger Menu
Salisbury steak with French Onion Sauce
Rice
Sautéed Zucchini
Fresh fruit

What will we do today?
- Review basic knife safety and knife skills
- Review basic food safety
- Discuss Sauté and Browning Technique
- Prepare Salisbury Steak menu
- Practice knife skills while preparing our menu
- Enjoy our menu

Clean, Separate, Cook, and Chill

Food safety is the most important factor in cooking. It doesn't matter how delicious or complicated your recipe is; if the food makes people sick because of improper cooking or handling, all your efforts will be wasted. You can't always tell if a food is safe to eat by how it looks or tastes. Proper storage, cooking, and handling are the only ways to ensure safe food.

Kitchen Primer: Dinner's Ready — participant handout

Safe steps in food handling, cooking, and storage are essential to prevent food-borne illness. You can't see, smell, or taste harmful bacteria that may cause illness.

The United States Department of Agriculture (USDA) uses four simple words to help you remember food safety rules, and we'll learn one more. They are **clean**, **separate**, **cook**, and **chill**. Let's learn about each term.

- **Clean** — Wash hands and surfaces often.
- **Separate** — Don't cross-contaminate.
- **Cook** — Cook to proper temperatures.
- **Chill** — Refrigerate promptly.
- **Caution** — Be cautious around heat and sharp tools.

Clean

It is important to keep your hands and all surfaces clean before, during, and after handling food.

Separate

Cross-contamination is the scientific word that describes the process of bacteria spreading from one food product to another. There is a high risk of this happening when people handle raw meat, poultry, and seafood, so keep these foods and their juices away from ready-to-eat and other raw foods such as produce.

It's really important to ensure that you do not introduce bacteria from raw meats, fish, and poultry to raw produce. This means you should always make sure to thoroughly clean your work area after handling different types of ingredients. This helps ensure that you don't cross-contaminate your ingredients.

- Separate raw meat, poultry, and seafood from other foods in your grocery shopping cart and in your refrigerator.
- If possible, use a different cutting board for raw meat products than you use for preparing produce and other foods.
- Always wash hands, cutting boards, dishes, and utensils with hot soapy water after they come in contact with raw meat, poultry, and seafood.
- Make sure to wash and disinfect your work area after preparing raw meat, fish, or poultry, and before handling other raw or cooked foods(for example, lettuce and tomatoes for salad).
- Never place cooked food on a plate which previously held raw meat, poultry, or seafood.

There are several places besides your work area where you have to be careful to avoid cross contamination. Here are some examples:

- When shopping, don't put raw produce, vegetables, and lettuces near raw meat in your shopping cart.
- Cooked food, packaged foods, and produce should always be placed on higher refrigerator shelves than raw meats, fish and poultry. Separating food this way ensures that any drippings from meat, fish or poultry don't contaminate the other foods.

Cook

Always cook food to the correct temperatures. It is particularly important to cook meats, fish, and poultry correctly to ensure that all bacteria are killed. Food safety experts agree that foods are properly cooked when they are heated for a long enough time and at a high enough temperature to kill the harmful bacteria that cause food-borne illness.

- Use a clean thermometer, which measures the internal temperature of cooked foods, to make sure meat, poultry, casseroles, and other foods are cooked all the way through.
- Cook roasts and steaks to at least 145°F. Whole poultry should be cooked to 180°F for doneness.
- Cook ground beef to at least 160°F. Information from the Centers for Disease Control and Prevention (CDC) link eating undercooked, pink ground beef with a higher risk of illness. If a meat thermometer is not available, do not eat ground beef that is still pink inside.
- Cook eggs until the yolk and white are firm. Don't use recipes in which eggs remain raw or only partially cooked.
- Fish should be cooked until opaque and/or flakes easily with a fork.

Chill

Refrigerate foods quickly because cold temperatures keep harmful bacteria from growing and multiplying. Make sure to set your refrigerator no higher than 40°F and the freezer unit at 0°F. Check these temperatures occasionally with an appliance thermometer. Then fight bacteria (Fight BAC!™) by following these steps:

- Refrigerate or freeze perishables, prepared foods, and leftovers within two hours.
- Never defrost food at room temperature. Thaw food in the refrigerator, under cold running water, or in the microwave. Marinate foods in the refrigerator.
- Divide large amounts of leftovers into small, shallow containers for quick cooling in the refrigerator.
- Don't pack the refrigerator. Cool air must circulate to keep food safe.

Shopping Tips

- Purchase refrigerated or frozen items after selecting your non-perishables.
- Never choose meat or poultry in packaging that is torn or leaking.
- Do not buy food past "Sell-By," "Use-By," or other expiration dates.
- Put raw meat and poultry into a plastic bag so meat juices will not cross-contaminate ready-to-eat food or food that is eaten raw, such as vegetables or fruit.
- Plan to drive directly home from the grocery store. You may want to take a cooler with ice for the perishables.

Food Safety Exercise

Directions: Read the paragraph below, and fill in the missing letters for the words with empty spaces.

Whenever I start cooking, I always wash my **h** _ _ _ _. I always make sure my **h** _ _ _ is covered or out of the way. I take off my jacket, roll up my sleeves, and wear an **a** _ _ _ _ _ to help keep outside germs away from food I am preparing. I always **c** _ _ _ _ countertops and surfaces before preparing food. When I prepare specific food, I always make sure to **s** _ _ _ _ _ _ _ vegetables from raw meats. I always **w** _ _ _ fruits and vegetables before beginning. I always **c** _ _ _ _ perishable foods in the refrigerator before and after cooking. I always **c** _ _ _ food to the correct temperature to stop any bacteria from growing inside my food.

SEPARATE

DON'T CROSS CONTAMINATE

Cross-contamination

(*kros \ken-tamé-ná shen*) is the scientific word for how bacteria are spread from one food product to another. This is especially true when handling raw meat, poultry and seafood, so keep these foods and their juices away from ready-to-eat foods!

CAN YOU FIND THE FOOD HANDLING MISTAKES?

DID YOU SEE THE KNIFE I WAS USING?

(UH-OH!)

WHERE'S THE SOAP?

NOT COOKED YET!

Just another typical day in an average household where many mistakes can be made when handling food! Circle all the mistakes, and learn to be a safe food handler! (The answers can be found by reading "Here's How to Fight BAC!™")

Here's How To Fight BAC!™

•**Separate** raw meat, poultry and seafood from other foods in your grocery shopping cart and in your refrigerator.

•**If possible**, use a different cutting board for raw meat products.

•**Always** wash hands, cutting boards, dishes and utensils with hot, soapy water after they come in contact with raw meat, poultry and seafood.

• **Never** place cooked food on a plate which previously held raw meat, poultry and seafood.

REMEMBER...
WASH YOUR HANDS WITH HOT, SOAPY WATER BEFORE HANDLING FOOD!

U.S. DEPARTMENT OF AGRICULTURE

WORD SEARCH

```
C Y S S C I E N C E E E E
O R D S O A P Y R C N T Q
I W I C O H Q B O L C A T
E A S U S I C K S E E R T
H S I T W E T C S A R A R
D H N T K C E O C N O P E
U H F I G H T U O P S E T
T A E N G B T N N L S S A
A N C G E A F T T A E P W
E D T B G C P E A T A Y T
M S S O T T O R M E F Y O
W A A A S E U S I E O D H
A D F R S R L E N I O A Y
R O E D C I T R A S D S X
R L R O F A G H T C I M R
Y R T L U O P C E I E T L
```

WORD BANK:
RAW MEAT
WASH HANDS
CROSS CONTAMINATE
CLEAN PLATE
CUTTING BOARD
DISINFECT
SEPARATE
FIGHT
BACTERIA
POULTRY
COUNTERS
SCIENCE
SAFE
SEAFOOD
SOAPY
HOT WATER
SICK

FIGHT BAC! Keep Food Safe from Bacteria™

Sauté and browning technique

What is sautéing?

One technique for cooking is called "sautéing". Sauté is a French word, and the literal translation in French is "to jump" (from the verb, sauter). When sautéing items; chefs will "toss" the food in a pan in such a way that its contents fly through the air, turn over and fall back into the pan. The food is cooked quickly in a small amount of oil or other fat in a skillet or sauté pan over direct heat.

How to sauté

- Before you begin to sauté, it is important to have everything prepared and located near the stove.

- Put the pan on the burner and turn burner to medium high heat. Allow the pan to heat; it should not be cold when you add oil or food to it.

- When the skillet is hot, add enough oil to thinly coat the bottom of the pan. Too little oil may make food cook unevenly and stick to the pan.

- When the oil is hot, add the food carefully to the pan.

- You're Sautéing!

What is browning?

Another technique is called "browning". Browning is a cooking technique that allows a meat or vegetable to become seared quickly over medium high heat. Usually it gets brown marks from the heat of the pan. Typically, after browning liquid is added to the pan to bring up flavors from the bits attached to the pan. The ingredient is then simmered slowly to finish cooking.

Day 2: Let's Cook

It's not just a Hamburger

Menu

Salisbury steak with French Onion Sauce
Rice
Sautéed Zucchini
Fresh fruit

Game plan

1. Prepare vegetables for each recipe and set aside
2. Prepare the fresh fruit and refrigerate or leave out at room temperature.
3. Begin cooking rice.
4. Follow Salisbury steak recipe.
5. Make the onion sauce in the skillet used for Salisbury steak recipe. The meat drippings flavor the sauce.
6. Keep steak in a warm 325° oven while preparing the remainder of the meal.
7. Sauté zucchini when sauce is almost done simmering.
8. When rice and zucchini are done, remove from heat & place in serving bowl
9. Set the table
10. Enjoy meal
11. Serve fresh fruit
12. Clear table
13. Clean up

Recipe

Salisbury steak with French Onion Sauce

Serves 12

Ingredients Salisbury Steak

Steaks:

- 3-pound ground beef (Beef, ground, 85% lean meat / 15% fat, raw)
- ½ cup fresh parsley chopped
- 6 Tbsp scallions finely chopped
- 2 tsp salt
- ½ tsp black pepper
- 2 Tbsp whole wheat flour
- 1 Tbsp olive oil

Optional garnish: parmesan cheese

Directions

1. Preheat oven to 325° oven
2. Combine meat, parsley, scallions, salt & pepper
3. Divide evenly into 12 portions and shape into patties ¾- to 1-inch thick patties.
4. Place flour in shallow bowl or plate and dredge each patty in flour
5. Heat oil in large pan over medium-high heat.
6. Add patties and sauté 3 minutes each side, until browned
7. Remove from pans and place in a roasting pan. Keep warm in the oven while preparing the rest of the dish.
8. Reserve pan for preparing Onion Sauce. (Do not wash!)

Ingredients – Onion Sauce

Sauce:

- 4 medium onions sliced
- 4 garlic cloves minced
- 3 Tbsp. tomato paste
- 2 Tbsp whole wheat flour
- 4 cups broth (beef or vegetarian – Low sodium)
- 1 tsp salt
- 1 tsp dried thyme leaves or1 tablespoon chopped fresh thyme leaves

Directions

1. Add onions to pan; sauté 5 minutes
2. Stir in garlic and tomato paste; sauté 1 minute more
3. Sprinkle with excess flour into pan, sauté 1 minute more
4. Whisk in broth, salt and thyme
5. Return meat to pan and bring broth to a boil
6. Reduce heat to medium and cover. Simmer 10 minutes.
7. Place a steak and spoonful of onion sauce on plate
8. Garnish with parsley & parmesan (optional)
9. Repeat for remaining servings.

Nutritional Values

Nutrient name	Nutrient value	Unit
Calories	290	
Total Fat	18	g
Saturated Fat	7	g
Trans Fat	1	g
Cholesterol	75	mg
Sodium	720	mg
Carbohydrates	7	g
Dietary Fiber	1	g
Sugars	3	g
Protein	24	g
Vitamin A	--	IU
Vitamin C	--	mg
Calcium	--	mg
Iron	--	mg

This dish qualifies for USDA Low calories with a portion size of 290g and meals and main dishes of 120 calories or less per 100g.

Recipe

Basic Rice

Serves 8

Ingredients

- 2 cups uncooked rice choose Jasmine or Basmati long grain rice (or try brown rice)
- 4 cups water
- ¼ tsp salt

Directions

1. Place water and salt in a 2-quart pot, cover and bring to boil over high heat
2. When water is boiling, add rice, stir, cover pot and reduce heat to low
3. Cook for 20 minutes

Note: Do not peek at rice; leave it covered so steam will not escape from the pot..

Nutritional Values for white rice

Nutrient name	Nutrient value	Unit
Calories	170	
Total Fat	0	g
Saturated Fat	0	g
Trans Fat	0	g
Cholesterol	0	mg
Sodium	55	mg
Carbohydrates	37	g
Dietary Fiber	< 1	g
Sugars	0	g
Protein	3	g
Vitamin A	--	IU
Vitamin C	--	mg
Calcium	--	mg
Iron	--	mg

Nutritional Values for brown rice

Nutrient name	Nutrient value	Unit
Calories	170	
Total Fat	0	g
Saturated Fat	0	g
Trans Fat	0	g
Cholesterol	0	mg
Sodium	75	mg
Carbohydrates	36	g
Dietary Fiber	2	g
Sugars	0	g
Protein	4	g
Vitamin A	--	IU
Vitamin C	--	mg
Calcium	--	mg
Iron	--	mg

% Daily Values are based on a 2000 calorie diet

Using brown rice for this dish qualifies for USDA low total fat, saturated fat free, cholesterol free, and sugar free.

Sautéed Zucchini

Serves 4

Ingredients

- 2 medium zucchinis
- 1 Tbsp olive oil
- 1 garlic clove coarsely chopped
- 1/8 tsp salt and pepper or to taste

Directions

1. Wash and dry zucchini
2. Quarter zucchini and slice the quarters into 1-inch pieces
3. Heat a 10- to 12-inch sauté pan over medium-high heat.
4. Add olive oil
5. Add zucchini and sauté for 3-4 minutes until softened but not mushy.
6. Add garlic and sauté 1-2 minutes longer.
7. Season with salt and pepper to taste and serve immediately.

Nutritional Values

Nutrient name	Nutrient value	Unit
Calories	45	
Total Fat	3.5	g
Saturated Fat	0.5	g
Trans Fat	0	g
Cholesterol	0	mg
Sodium	50	mg
Carbohydrates	4	g
Dietary Fiber	1	g
Sugars	2	g
Protein	1	g
Vitamin A	--	IU
Vitamin C	--	mg
Calcium	--	mg
Iron	--	mg

This dish qualifies for USDA low calories, total saturated fat, cholesterol free, and low sodium.

Winter Options:

If zucchini is not in season, you may be able to use broccoli, Swiss chard, kale, or Brussels sprouts. You may roast vegetables like broccoli, or Brussels sprouts – see recipe Day 4.

Fresh Fruit

Serves 4

Ingredients

- ¼ pound fruit per person

Directions

1. Wash, dry, and slice fruit onto a platter for serving.

Sample fruit combinations:

- Assorted berries like strawberries, blueberries, raspberries, and blackberries.

- Melon, like cantaloupe, and honeydew

- Exotic fruit, like mango, pineapple, and bananas

- Stone fruit, like plums, nectarines, peaches, and apricots.

- Fall fruit, like apples, bananas and pears.

- Winter fruit, like bananas, oranges, nectarines, and kiwi.

Nutrition varies by type of fruit

Course: *Kitchen Primer: Dinner's Ready*
Day 3

Day 3 overview

Overview

Description

You will learn the importance of planning for meals in a day to help meet MyPlate guidelines for eating the recommended food groups. You will also learn about quick and nutrition ways to serve pasta.

Objectives

- Understand the basic components of a balanced meal
- Understand how planning for the meals in a day can help meet MyPlate guidelines for eating the recommended food groups
- Participants practice cooking techniques while preparing the menu for the day.

Everyone likes Pasta Menu

Pasta with seasonal sauce
Simple Salad
Italian Style Green Beans

What will we do today?

- Review MyPlate and the food groups
- Learn how to plan a balanced meal
- As a group discuss the case study and as a group complete the menu1 and menu2 comparison
- Prepare our menu
- Enjoy our menu

Sum of the Parts Equals a Meal

Overview

This lesson will teach what types of food make a plate healthy. Using 10 tips from the USDA MyPlate recommendations we will learn how to make a meal balanced, nutritious, and tasty.

What's A Balanced Plate?

If you are planning breakfast, lunch, or dinner, it is important to plan a balanced meal so that you get all nutrients your body needs to function properly. To make a balanced meal include at least one food from each of the following categories:

- Protein & Dairy, which include beans, nuts, meat, eggs, milk, and yogurt
- unrefined starches like whole grain bread or pasta
- Vitamin and mineral-rich foods, which include vegetables and fruit

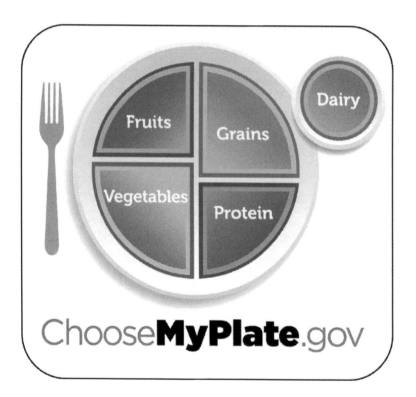

As a reminder here are the 5 basic food groups:
1) Dairy
2) Fruit
3) Grains
4) Protein Foods
5) Vegetables

Over the course of the day, make sure you have plenty of the various kinds of food so you stay healthy. You should eat breakfast, lunch, and dinner and sometimes snacks.

Most everyday family meals should be quick and easy, because everyone is busy going to work, school, and after-school activities. Dinners should include a salad, a main course, and a simple dessert. For special occasions and holidays, you might add appetizers, which are really a type of snack, and a fancier dessert.

Build A Healthy Meal Worksheet

10 tips

Nutrition Education Series

choose MyPlate

10 tips to a great plate

ChooseMyPlate.gov

Making food choices for a healthy lifestyle can be as simple as using these 10 Tips.
Use the ideas in this list to *balance your calories*, to choose foods to *eat more often*, and to cut back on foods to *eat less often*.

1 balance calories
Find out how many calories YOU need for a day as a first step in managing your weight. Go to www.ChooseMyPlate.gov to find your calorie level. Being physically active also helps you balance calories.

2 enjoy your food, but eat less
Take the time to fully enjoy your food as you eat it. Eating too fast or when your attention is elsewhere may lead to eating too many calories. Pay attention to hunger and fullness cues before, during, and after meals. Use them to recognize when to eat and when you've had enough.

3 avoid oversized portions
Use a smaller plate, bowl, and glass. Portion out foods before you eat. When eating out, choose a smaller size option, share a dish, or take home part of your meal.

4 foods to eat more often
Eat more vegetables, fruits, whole grains, and fat-free or 1% milk and dairy products. These foods have the nutrients you need for health—including potassium, calcium, vitamin D, and fiber. Make them the basis for meals and snacks.

5 make half your plate fruits and vegetables
Choose red, orange, and dark-green vegetables like tomatoes, sweet potatoes, and broccoli, along with other vegetables for your meals. Add fruit to meals as part of main or side dishes or as dessert.

6 switch to fat-free or low-fat (1%) milk
They have the same amount of calcium and other essential nutrients as whole milk, but fewer calories and less saturated fat.

7 make half your grains whole grains
To eat more whole grains, substitute a whole-grain product for a refined product—such as eating whole-wheat bread instead of white bread or brown rice instead of white rice.

8 foods to eat less often
Cut back on foods high in solid fats, added sugars, and salt. They include cakes, cookies, ice cream, candies, sweetened drinks, pizza, and fatty meats like ribs, sausages, bacon, and hot dogs. Use these foods as occasional treats, not everyday foods.

9 compare sodium in foods
Use the Nutrition Facts label to choose lower sodium versions of foods like soup, bread, and frozen meals. Select canned foods labeled "low sodium," "reduced sodium," or "no salt added."

10 drink water instead of sugary drinks
Cut calories by drinking water or unsweetened beverages. Soda, energy drinks, and sports drinks are a major source of added sugar, and calories, in American diets.

United States Department of Agriculture Center for Nutrition Policy and Promotion

DG TipSheet No. 1
June 2011
USDA is an equal opportunity provider and employer.

Go to www.ChooseMyPlate.gov for more information.

Optional Exercise

After reviewing MyPlate take a few minutes to write down a typical day's menu for you.   If you need additional space, use the blank space at the bottom of the page.

Breakfast

What do you normally have for breakfast in the morning?

_____   _____   _____

Lunch

What is a typical lunch you might eat during school?

_____   _____   _____

Snack

Do you have a snack after school? What might you eat for a snack?

_____   _____

Dinner

What do you eat at dinner time?

_____   _____   _____

Case Study – Checking your foods daily

Most of you are familiar with MyPlate and the different food groups. Today we will tie the food groups to our daily meals. Food is necessary to help us grow during childhood and teen years and to sustain adults. Food and water keep our body engine running. Eating the correct quantities throughout the day helps us stay healthy. It's important to understand how to eat throughout the day.

According to a sample MyPlate worksheet, a 7-year-old boy who exercises moderately is supposed to have the following foods daily:

5 oz. of grains	2 ½ cups of the milk group
2 cups of vegetables	5 oz. of the meat and bean group
1 ½ cups of fruits	

Kitchen Primer Dinner's Ready —participant handout

Note the following two menu choices and complete the exercises below.

1. Menu choice 1	2. Menu choice 2
a. Breakfast	a. Breakfast
• 1 pancake (2 oz.) with 2 tbsp. syrup	• breakfast cereal (2 oz)
• 1 cup of milk	• 1 cup of milk
b. Lunch	b. Lunch
• 1 turkey (2 oz.) sandwich on white bread (3 oz.) with mayonnaise	• 1 turkey (2 oz.) and cheese (1/4 cup) sandwich on whole wheat bread (3 oz.), slice of tomato, and piece of lettuce (1/4 cup)
• 1 bag of potato chips	• 1 apple
• 1 apple	• 1 oatmeal cookie (1/2oz.)
c. After school snack	c. After school snack
• 1 soda — 10 oz.	• 1 corn tortilla (1/2 oz.)
• 1 bag of corn chips	• Chopped peppers and onions (1/2 cup)
	• ¼ cup of cheese
d. Dinner	d. Dinner
• 2 pieces of fried chicken (6 oz.)	• Green salad (1/2 cup)
• French fries (1 cup)	• 1-piece roasted chicken (3 oz.)
• Broccoli (1/2 cup)	• Broccoli (¾ cup)
	• Baked potato (1/2 cup)
	• 1 cup of frozen yogurt

Case Study Questions

Exercise: Use the menu choices 1 and 2 to answer the following:

1. Does Menu 1 have a meal that has the three categories of food that make up a healthy plate? _____

2. List any of the foods in Menu 1 that represent the following food groups below.

   - Protein: _____

   - Carbohydrate: _____

   - Vitamin/Mineral-Rich Food: _____

3. How many ounces of the protein group does Menu choice 1 have? _____

4. Does Menu 1 have any lean proteins?

   _____

5. What category of food is missing for dinner in Menu 1? _____

6. List a food that would make Menu1 dinner balanced.

   _____

7. Which meals from Menu 2 have a balanced plate?

   _____

   _____

   _____

8. What fruit is on Menu 2? _____

9. What meal could you easily add fruit to?

   _____

   _____

   _____

10. How many ounces of the grain group does Menu choice 2 have?

_____

11. What foods in Menu 2 are whole-grains?

_____

_____

12. How many servings are there from the dairy group in Menu 2?

_____

13. What types of dairy foods should you choose to make a healthy plate?

_____

_____

14. Bonus: According to a sample MyPlate worksheet, a 7-year-old is supposed to have the following foods daily:

5 oz. of grains
2 cups of vegetables
1 ½ cups of fruits
2 1/2 cups of the milk group
5 oz. of the meat and bean group

15. Looking at the two menu choices, circle the one that meets the MyPlate recommendation for a 7-year-old boy?

Menu Choice 1   Menu Choice 2

P is for Pasta

Dry and fresh pasta

Pasta can be purchased fresh or dried. Typically, spaghetti is a dry pasta, while fettuccine is often found fresh. Generally Northern Italy uses more fresh pasta and Southern Italy uses more dry pasta.

Dry pastas are made using flour and water. The best dry pasta is made with the inner part of the wheat called durum, known as durum semolina when ground. The high gluten content in the flour helps the pasta soften yet remain firm when cooked, al dente.

Fresh pasta has a lighter texture because it is made with flour, eggs and water. It's not quite as easy to find fresh pasta as dried pasta. Wonton wrappers are pretty common in California and can be used as fresh pasta. Or, learn to make your own!

Cooking pasta

Bring a large pot of water to boil. Plan at least 4-5 quarts of water for 1 pound of pasta. Pasta will not cook properly if there is too little water. Traditionally, it is not necessary to add oil. Oil is sometimes added to ensure the pasta does not stick together; however, oil also will prevent the sauce from sticking to the pasta. So Chef-K does not recommend adding oil to pasta water.

When the water is boiling, add about 2-3 teaspoons of salt and then add the pasta. Give it a stir with a wooden spoon to prevent it from sticking.

Tasting the pasta is the best way to determine the doneness. Many packaged pasta instructions result in overcooked pasta, particularly because the pasta continues to cook as it is drained. Shape, size, fresh or dry all impact the cooking time needed. Strands like Cappelli or angel hair take only 1-2 minutes. Other dry pasta like pappardelle, spaghetti, rigatoni should be tested for doneness at five minutes. It should be firm, yet tender. The longest-cooking pastas should be done within 10-12 minutes.

Since pasta continues to cook, it is critical to drain it quickly, so have a colander in your clean sink ready to drain the instant it is al dente. Give the colander a couple of vigorous shakes to drain well and then pour into a serving bowl.

DAY 3: Let's Cook

Everyone likes Pasta

Menu

Pasta with seasonal sauce
Simple Salad
Italian Style Green Beans
Fresh Fruit

Game plan

1. Heat pot of water for blanching tomatoes
2. Prepare salad ingredients
3. Prepare green bean ingredients
4. Prepare ingredients for tomato sauce per recipe
5. Heat pot of water for pasta
6. Cook tomato sauce
7. Make Green Sauce
8. Cook Green beans
9. Cook pasta
10. Assemble salad
11. Drain pasta and add red sauce to ½ of cooked pasta
12. Add green sauce to other ½ of cooked pasta
13. Dress Salad
14. Serve meal

Recipe: Pasta with Red and Green Sauce

Red sauce – summer tomato

Makes 1 quart

Ingredients

- 4 pounds fresh ripe plum tomatoes
- 4 Tbsp olive oil
- 2 medium onions peeled and halved
- ¼ tsp salt
- ¼ tsp black pepper

Directions

1. Bring a large pot of water to boil
2. Blanch tomatoes in boiling water for about 3 minutes
3. Rinse in cold water, drain, and peel tomatoes
4. Cut tomatoes in half, remove seeds and chop
5. Add tomatoes to a heavy 5-quart saucepan over medium heat
6. Add olive oil, onion, salt and pepper
7. When it begins to bubble, reduce heat to low and simmer for 30-45 minutes
8. Break up tomatoes with potato masher or slotted spoon as they cook.
9. Discard onion
10. Taste and add salt and pepper as necessary.

Note: If desired, puree tomato to smoother sauce in a food processor or with an immersion blender. It's okay to puree onions with sauce at kid chef's discretion.

Winter Options:

You can replace fresh tomatoes with a 32 oz can of low salt whole tomatoes. Skip steps 1-5 of the directions if you use canned tomatoes.

You can also sauté some fresh mushrooms with a garlic clove and parsley to garnish the tomato sauce over pasta.

Nutritional Values

Nutrient name	Nutrient value	Unit
Calories	110	
Total Fat	10	g
Saturated Fat	1.5	g
Trans Fat	0	g
Cholesterol	0	mg
Sodium	75	mg
Carbohydrates	4	g
Dietary Fiber	<1	g
Sugars	3	g
Protein	<1	g
Vitamin A		IU
Vitamin C		mg
Calcium		mg
Iron		mg

This dish qualifies for USDA cholesterol free, and low sodium

Green Sauce (Pesto) – Summer only

Makes 1½ cups

This pesto is based on the traditional Genoa style. The traditional recipe includes pine nuts; however, you may substitute blanched almonds instead.

Ingredients

- 4 cups fresh basil leaves
- ¼ cup blanched almonds or pine nuts, optionally toasted
- 4 cloves garlic
- 1 tsp salt
- ¼ to ½ cup olive oil
- ¾ to 1 cup Parmesan or other dry cheese, grated

Directions

1. Gently wash and spin dry the basil leaves.
2. Put the basil, pine nuts, garlic, and salt in a blender or food processor.
3. Mix at high speed, periodically scraping down the sides, and slowly pour in olive oil until a fine paste is achieved.
4. Transfer the sauce to a small bowl and mix in cheese by hand until blended.

Note: If you would like to store basil for future use, it can be frozen. Here's how: purée only the basil leaves. Put the puréed basil in ice cube trays, pour olive oil over to cover, and freeze. Once the basil is frozen, transfer it to zippered plastic freezer bags. Each cube equals about 1 tablespoon of basil. Add the frozen cubes while sautéing vegetables or making soups or stews. You can thaw the cubes and add the remaining ingredients to make pesto.

Winter Options:

It's usually difficult to find fresh basil in non-summer months; so you will have to skip the pesto recipe.

Nutrition Facts

Nutrient name	Nutrient value	Unit
Calories	170	—
Total fat	16	g
Saturated fat	4	g
Trans fat	0	g
Cholesterol	10	mg
Sodium	590	mg
Carbohydrate	2	g
Dietary fiber	0	g
Sugars	0	g
Protein	6	g
Vitamin A	—	IU
Vitamin C	—	mg
Calcium	—	mg
Iron	—	mg

This dish qualifies for USDA low cholesterol, and sugar free.

Recipe: Pasta for 8

Ingredients

- 1-pound whole grain Fusilli or pappardelle or other small dry pasta with "pockets" or ridges. (or standard white flour pasta if whole grain is not available)
- 1 Tbsp olive oil
- 1/8 tsp salt and pepper to taste
- 2 Tbsp Parmesan cheese grated

From recipes above:

- ½ cup pesto
- 2 cups tomato sauce

Directions

1. Bring 6-8-quart pot of water to boil.
2. Add olive oil. Cook pasta 10-12 minutes. Usually package instructions overcook the pasta to my taste, so set timer for 2 minutes before package directions and taste. Pasta should be al dente (in other words has a little bite inside) Pasta continues to cook as you drain and prepare it.
3. When al dente, drain pasta in a large strainer.
4. Pour pasta into a bowl and add tomato sauce, salt and pepper and cheese to taste.

Nutrition Facts for standard white flour pasta

Nutrient name	Nutrient value	Unit
Calories	280	—
Total fat	9	g
Saturated fat	2	g
Trans fat	0	g
Cholesterol	5	mg
Sodium	160	mg
Carbohydrate	43	g
Dietary fiber	2	g
Sugars	1	g
Protein	9	g
Vitamin A	—	IU
Vitamin C	—	mg
Calcium	—	mg
Iron	—	mg

Nutrition Facts for whole grain pasta

Nutrient name	Nutrient value	Unit
Calories	280	—
Total fat	9	g
Saturated fat	2	g
Trans fat	0	g
Cholesterol	5	mg
Sodium	160	mg
Carbohydrate	42	g
Dietary fiber	6	g
Sugars	2	g
Protein	9	g
Vitamin A	—	IU
Vitamin C	—	mg
Calcium	—	mg
Iron	—	mg

When using whole grain pasta, this dish qualifies for USDA low cholesterol, and sugar free.

Recipe: Simple Salad

Serves 6

Ingredients

¼ red Italian-style torpedo onion (other sweet red onions are ok)
1 stalk celery
2 cups spring greens (about 8 oz)
1 small tomato or ½ basket of cherry tomatoes, or pear or apple diced in winter
Salt (1/8 tsp to start)
2 Tbsp olive oil
2 Tbsp + 1 Tbsp red wine vinegar or white wine vinegar

Directions

1. Peel the onion and slice it in thin semicircles.
2. Place the onion in a small bowl, add 1 tablespoon of vinegar, and cover with cold water. Let it sit while you prepare the rest of the salad.
3. Wash and dry the celery and cut it into thin semicircles.
4. Wash the spring greens and spin them in a salad spinner or pat them dry with a paper towel.
5. Trim the spring greens, if needed.
6. Wash the tomato or fruit, and then cut in half and slice each half into pieces.
7. Drain the onions.
8. Put all of the ingredients into a large bowl.
9. When ready to serve, add salt and olive oil, and gently toss.
10. Sprinkle with vinegar, and gently toss once more.
11. Serve immediately.

Winter Options:

Eliminate tomato, replace with pear or apple.

Spring Options:

Eliminate tomato, replace with radishes.

Nutrition Facts

Nutrient name	Nutrient value	Unit
Calories	340	—
Total fat	28	g
Saturated fat	4	g
Trans fat	0	g
Cholesterol	0	mg
Sodium	410	mg
Carbohydrate	20	g
Dietary fiber	7	g
Sugars	10	g
Protein	6	g
Vitamin A	—	IU
Vitamin C	—	mg
Calcium	—	mg
Iron	—	mg

This dish qualifies for USDA low calories, low sodium, and cholesterol free.

Recipe: Italian-style Green Beans

Serves 6

The trick to tasty green beans is to choose beans that are smaller, bright green and firm. Larger beans that are not firm will be stringy and tough. Make sure to cook them just until they are tender but still a little firm.

Ingredients

- 1 pound green beans
- 2 Tbsp olive oil
- 1 clove garlic, minced (optional)
- Salt and pepper to taste (1/8 tsp of each to start)

Directions

1. Break off ends of beans and rinse in cold water.
2. Bring 3 quarts of water to a boil in a 4-5-quart pot.
3. Add the beans and pour in additional water if the beans are not completely covered. Cook until tender but still firm, about 4–5 minutes.
4. Drain the beans and place in a serving bowl.
5. Drizzle with olive oil and sprinkle with garlic, salt and pepper.

Note: If green beans are tough, you can blanch them in boiling water for a few minutes.

Nutritional Values

Nutrient name	Nutrient value	Unit
Calories	60	
Total Fat	4.5	g
Saturated Fat	0.5	g
Trans Fat	0	g
Cholesterol	0	mg
Sodium	55	mg
Carbohydrates	5	g
Dietary Fiber	3	g
Sugars	1	g
Protein	1	g
Vitamin A		IU
Vitamin C		mg
Calcium		mg
Iron		mg

This dish qualifies for USDA low calories, low saturated fat, low sodium, and cholesterol free.

Winter Options:

If green beans are not in season, you may be able to use broccoli, Swiss chard, kale, or Brussels sprouts. You may roast vegetables like broccoli, or Brussels sprouts – see recipe Day 4.

Fresh Fruit

Serves 4

Ingredients

- ¼ pound fruit per person

Directions

2. Rinse, dry, and slice fruit onto a platter for serving.

Sample fruit combinations:

- Assorted berries like strawberries, blueberries, raspberries, and blackberries.

- Melon, like cantaloupe, and honey dew

- Exotic fruit, like mango, pineapple, and bananas

- Stone fruit, like plums, nectarines, peaches, and apricots.

- Fall fruit, like apples, bananas, and pears.

- Winter fruit, like bananas, oranges, nectarines, and kiwi.

Nutrition varies by type of fruit

Course: Kitchen Primer: Dinner's Ready
Day 4

Day 4 overview

Description

You will learn about common food allergies, and the causes and symptoms of a food allergy. You will learn the 8 foods that most often cause food allergies.

Objectives

After completing this class, you will be able to:

- describe what a food allergy is
- Become aware of what to look for on food labels as it pertains to food allergies
- Describe cooking food in the oven

Basic Roasted Meal Menu

Oven roasted chicken with potatoes

Roasted seasonal vegetables

What will we do today?

- Review top food allergies
- Learn about cooking in the oven
- Prepare our menu
- Enjoy our menu

Food Allergies

Today we are talking about food allergies. Are you allergic to anything? Is anyone in your household allergic to something? What kinds of things are they allergic to?

What is a food allergy?

A food allergy is an adverse reaction to a food or an ingredient in a food component that involves the body's immune system. Usually a protein causes a food allergy. It can be a serious condition and should be diagnosed by a board-certified allergist. A true food allergy (also called "food hypersensitivity") and its symptoms can take many forms. Common reactions are listed below, in the section titled "How to recognize a food allergy."

How does the body react to a food allergy?

A food allergy reaction usually occurs immediately or within 2 hours of contact with the offending food. Reactions can range from mild to life threatening. In a true food allergy, the body mistakenly identifies a food or a substance in food as a harmful substance, and the immune system forms antibodies to fight the culprit food or food substance (the allergen). The next time there is food contact, the antibodies release a chemical called histamine, as well as other chemicals, into your bloodstream. This leads to the allergic reaction. A person does not have to eat the food to experience an allergic reaction. Exposure to the food can be from inhalation, ingestion, or skin contact with the offending food.

What are the foods that most often cause food allergies?

There are 8 foods that most often cause allergies and generally these foods are high in protein. They are:
- milk
- eggs
- peanuts
- tree nuts (such as pecans or almonds)
- soy
- wheat
- fish
- shellfish

The most common childhood food allergy is milk although most outgrow this allergy by age three. The most serious allergic reactions are from peanuts and tree nuts. Allergies to peanuts and tree nuts are not generally outgrown.

Many of these foods are contained within other processed foods. It is very important to read the food labels on products to determine if any offending foods are contained within another product. For example, if a child was allergic to soy, products should be avoided that contain hydrolyzed soy protein, soy sauce, tofu, or textured vegetable protein. Even in very small amounts, an allergic reaction could occur if a person is exposed to these.

To help Americans avoid the health risks posed by food allergens, Congress passed the **Food Allergen Labeling and Consumer Protection Act of 2004**. This law requires that food labels must clearly identify the source of all ingredients that are — or are derived from — the eight most common food allergens. As a result, food labels will help allergic consumers to identify offending foods or ingredients so they can more easily avoid them.

Who is affected by food allergies?

Food allergy frequency is increasing in children. Currently about 4-8% of children have allergies. Infants under 2 years of age are more likely to develop food allergies but the incidence decreases with age. Some children grow out of food allergies. Factors that may increase chances for food allergies include heredity, exposure to allergens, gastrointestinal permeability, and environmental factors. About 2% of the adult population has food allergies.

How do you recognize a food allergy?

There are different types of allergic reactions to food. Allergic reactions can include:

- Hives

- Flushed skin or rash

- Tingling or itchy sensation in the mouth

- Face, tongue, or lip swelling

- Vomiting and/or diarrhea

- Coughing or wheezing

- Dizziness and/or lightheadedness

- Swelling of the throat and vocal cords

- Difficulty breathing

- Loss of consciousness

- Abdominal cramps

In rare cases of severe allergies, anaphylactic shock occurs. This includes multiple allergic reactions such as itching, hives, swelling of the throat, difficulty breathing, lower blood pressure, and loss of consciousness. Emergency medical treatment is needed immediately. Anaphylactic shock accounts for about 200 deaths per year.

What is the treatment for a food allergy?

The only way to avoid food allergies is to strictly avoid the offending food. Some children grow out of their allergies, so often a food that was once an allergy source may be reintroduced into the diet to determine if the allergic response is still active.

It is important to read all food labels carefully. A person that is severely allergic to certain foods should carry epinephrine, an important medication, with them at all times.

Tips to remember:

- Food allergies are serious. Don't make jokes about them.

- Don't share food with friends who have food allergies.

- Wash your hands after eating.

- Ask what your friends are allergic to, and help them avoid it.

Optional Group Activity

Do you ever look at the labels of the foods that you consume? By law, food packages must list all the ingredients in a product.

Ingredient lists tell you which ingredients are in the products you buy. This information is always printed on the outside of the package. Food ingredients are listed according to the amount of each ingredient in the package. The ingredient that weighs the most is listed first, and the ingredient that weighs the least is listed last.

Here is an example of an ingredient label for bread:

Whole Wheat Flour, Water, Wheat Gluten, Brown Sugar,
Molasses, Soybean Oil, Honey, Yeast, Salt, Cultured Wheat Starch, Oats, Soy Flour, Dough Conditioners.

Which ingredients may be a problem for people with food allergies? Which of the 8 foods that most often cause food allergies are contained in this bread?

What's in the oven?

Today we will be roasting meats and vegetables as well as baking some apples. Today we will be using the oven to prepare our meals. There are multiple styles of cooking in an oven. Here are a few:

- Roasting
- Baking
- Broiling

What is roasting?

As a young girl, the first meal I learned to make "all by myself" was roasted chicken with potatoes, onions and garlic served with a big green salad. It was an easy one pan meal. This became my specialty to make on Sundays, while my parents and brothers were out for the day.

Roasting is a specific method of baking food in the oven. It uses dry-heat with a minimum of fat, such as olive oil or butter at a high temperature. The only moisture is a bit that is naturally released from the food. The food will come out crisp and golden and flavorful.

Pans and heat

Meat should be roasted in a heavy metal roasting pans. Always use a roasting rack for meat so it does not steam in its own juices. Drain off some of the fat. Then deglaze the pan by pouring either lemon juice or wine to make a wonderful sauce to pour over the meat. Adding liquid to the pan lets you scrape up the brown bits and blends with the meat juices. This also makes it easier to clean the pan afterwards.

Vegetables should be roasted in either a heavy roasting pan or a heatproof glass baking dish with two- to three-inch sides. Use a pan that fits the amount of vegetables in a single layer. It's ok to layer the vegetables surrounding the meat rack. However, if you would like to reduce your intake of animal fat, place vegetables in a separate pan.

Day 4: Let's Cook

Basic Roasted Meal

Menu

Oven roasted chicken with potatoes

Roasted seasonal vegetables

Fresh fruit

Game plan

1. Preheat oven 425°
2. Prepare chicken
3. Place chicken in oven roast
4. Prepare vegetables, set aside
5. Prepare fruit and set aside
6. Add potatoes to chicken roasting pan (or a separate pan)
7. Prepare and roast seasonal vegetables
8. Remove chicken & vegetables let rest
9. Set table then carve chicken and serve meal
10. Clear table
11. Enjoy fresh Fruit

Recipe: *Roasted Chicken With Potatoes, Onions and Garlic*

Serves 12-15

> This is the way my family always prepared chicken. It's the easiest and most straight forward way to cook a chicken.
>
> A note from Laurie Zerga, founder of Chef-K

Ingredients

- 2 Whole chickens (4-7 pounds each.) Mary's or Organic chicken preferred
- 4-6 Tbsp olive oil divided
- 1 Tbs minced fresh rosemary or 1 teaspoon dried
- 4-6 garlic cloves minced
- 1/8 tsp salt & pepper
- 15 medium new potatoes or Yukon gold washed and quartered
- 2-3 medium onions peeled and quartered
- 8-9 whole garlic cloves peeled

Directions

1. Preheat oven to 425°
2. Remove neck and giblets from chicken. (Optional: reserve for making a quick stock)
3. Rinse chicken with cold water and pat dry with paper towels inside and out.
4. Salt and pepper body cavity.
5. Arrange on a roasting rack in a roasting pan
6. Brush the breast and legs with 2-3 Tbsp olive oil. Sprinkle with 1/8 tsp salt and pepper, and the rosemary
7. Brush minced garlic over chicken.
8. Place potatoes, onion and whole garlic around chicken and drizzle 2-3 Tbsp olive oil over vegetables. Salt and pepper to taste.
9. It will take 50-75 minutes to roast, depending on the size of the chicken. Use an instant-read meat thermometer to prick the thickest part of the thigh. It should register 160-170°. If the temperature is allowed to go higher; it will dry out the breast meat.
10. Remove chicken to a platter to let rest for 10-15 minutes; it will continue to cook from its own heat.
11. Remove leg & thighs & wings. Then carve breast and place on warm platter.
12. Place potatoes in a serving casserole and leave in warm oven.

Nutritional Values

Nutrient name	Nutrient value	Unit
Calories	560	
Total Fat	32	g
Saturated Fat	9	g
Trans Fat	0	g
Cholesterol	130	mg
Sodium	130	mg
Carbohydrates	32	g
Dietary Fiber	4	g
Sugars	2	g
Protein	34	g
Vitamin A		IU
Vitamin C		mg
Calcium		mg
Iron		mg

This dish qualifies for USDA low sodium.

Pan Gravy (optional)
Ingredients

- 1/4 cup fresh lemon juice
- 1/2 cup chicken stock or broth
- Drippings from the roasting pan

Directions

1. Drain off excess fat. Then place pan with drippings on stove burner.
2. Add wine or lemon juice, scraping up brown bits at bottom of pan.
3. Add chicken stock and bring to boil.
4. Reduce the heat and let simmer 10-15 minutes to reduce to a rich sauce.

Recipe: Roasted Vegetables

Excellent vegetables to roast include:

- Asparagus (10 minutes)
- Broccoli, (20 minutes)
- Brussels Sprouts (15 minutes)
- Cauliflower (20 minutes)
- Eggplant (sliced, 15 minutes)
- Kale (sliced, 10 minutes)
- Onions (sliced, 15 minutes)
- Peppers (15 minutes)
- Potatoes (40 minutes)
- Zucchini (1-inch pieces, 15 minutes)

Drizzle with:

- 2 Tbsp olive oil
- ¼ tsp each salt and pepper

Directions

1.   Preheat oven 400°

2. Rinse, dry, and slice vegetable of choice as desired

3. Drizzle 1-2 Tbsp olive oil over vegetables and roast for time specified above.

Note: try other herbs such as oregano or rosemary on potatoes or zucchini, or dill on cauliflower. Experiment!

Sample vegetable combinations:

- Broccoli and cauliflower.

- Beets and Zucchini (this is an unexpected combination and quite tasty)

- Carrots and cauliflower

- Carrots and Brussels sprouts

- Corn and peppers

- Zucchini, eggplant, and peppers

Nutrition information varies based on vegetables used.

Fresh Fruit

Serves 4

Ingredients

- ¼ pound fruit per person

Directions

Rinse , dry, and slice fruit onto a platter for serving.

Sample fruit combinations:

- Assorted berries like strawberries, blueberries, raspberries, and blackberries.
- Melon, like cantaloupe, and honeydew
- Exotic fruit, like mango, pineapple, and bananas
- Stone fruit, like plums, nectarines, peaches, and apricots.
- Fall fruit, like apples, bananas, and pears.
- Winter fruit, like bananas, oranges, nectarines, and kiwi.

Nutrition varies by type of fruit

Course: Kitchen Primer: Dinner's Ready
Day 5

Day 5 overview

Description

Celebrate what you have learned and enjoy a buffet.

Objectives

- Prepare a celebration buffet

Mexican Fiesta Menu

Turkey Tacos
Shredded Cheese
Guacamole
Salsa Fresca
Tortilla Chips
Warm Corn & Flour Tortillas
Calabacitas with Corn and Tomatoes
Fresh Fruit

What will we do today?

- Plan and prepare our celebration
- Prepare our menu
- Enjoy our dinner

Day 5: Let's Cook

Mexican Fiesta

Menu

Turkey Tacos
Guacamole
Salsa Fresca
Tortilla Chips
Calabacitas with Corn and Tomatoes
Fresh Fruit

Game plan

1. Prepare the vegetables for calabacitas and set aside.
2. Prepare the fruit for dessert.
3. Prepare salsa and guacamole, cover and set on table.
4. Prepare Turkey Tacos
5. Set the table and set out drinks.
6. Set out a buffet of food and serve.
7. Clear dishes from the table.

Recipe: Basic Table Salsa (Salsa Fresca)

Makes 1 ½ cups
Serves 8

Ingredients

- 2 large, firm red-ripe tomatoes seeded (or fresh cranberries in winter)
- 1 clove garlic peeled
- 1 Anaheim or California green chili seeded
- 3 green onions trimmed and chopped, or 1/3 cup chopped red onion
- 1 tsp olive oil
- 1 Tbsp fresh lime juice or wine vinegar
- ¼ tsp salt, or to taste
- Cracked black pepper
- 1 Tbsp chopped cilantro (optional)

Directions

1. Chop tomatoes and place in bowl.
2. Chop, garlic, chili, and onions together then add to tomatoes. (All ingredients should be chopped either by hand, in a blender, or food processor until desired consistency.)
3. Mix in green chilies, olive oil, lime juice, salt, pepper and cilantro.
4. Allow flavors to develop for 1 hour, and then serve.

Nutritional Values

Nutrient name	Nutrient value	Unit
Calories	20	
Total Fat	1.5	g
Saturated Fat	0	g
Trans Fat	0	g
Cholesterol	0	mg
Sodium	75	mg
Carbohydrates	1	g
Dietary Fiber	0	g
Sugars	< 1	g
Protein	0	g
Vitamin A	--	IU
Vitamin C	--	mg
Calcium	--	mg
Iron	--	mg

This dish qualifies for USDA low calories, free of saturated fat, and cholesterol free.

Winter Options:

Note: During winter – try replacing tomatoes with a 12 oz bag of fresh cranberries

Recipe: Guacamole

Makes 1 cup
Serves 8

Ingredients

- 4 ripe avocados mashed (if unavailable look for frozen avocados)
- 1 Tbsp fresh lime juice (or lemon if lime is not available, a combination is also fine)
- Salt & pepper to taste

Directions

1. Combine all ingredients.
2. To store, cover tightly with plastic wrap so that the avocadoes do not get dark and are less appetizing (It is okay to prepare several hours ahead and possibly the night before).

Nutritional Values

Nutrient name	Nutrient value	Unit
Calories	160	
Total Fat	15	g
Saturated Fat	2	g
Trans Fat	0	g
Cholesterol	0	mg
Sodium	25	mg
Carbohydrates	9	g
Dietary Fiber	7	g
Sugars	< 1	g
Protein	2	g
Vitamin A	--	IU
Vitamin C	--	mg
Calcium	--	mg
Iron	--	mg

This dish qualifies for USDA low sodium, and cholesterol free.

Recipe: Calabacitas with Corn and Tomatoes

Serves 6

Ingredients

- 3 Tbsp olive oil
- ½ medium onion, peeled and sliced into eighths
- 1 garlic clove peeled and coarsely chopped
- 1 yellow summer squash sliced 1-inch thick
- 1 small zucchini squash sliced 1-inch thick
- 3 green onions sliced
- ½ cup fresh or frozen corn kernels (from t 1 to 2 ears of fresh corn)
- 1 mild green chili, roasted, peeled, seeded, and cut into pieces
- 2 plum (Roma) tomatoes, quartered and seeded
- ⅛ tsp salt and pepper, or to taste

Directions

1. Pre heat oven to 400°F
2. Place onion, garlic, and squash on a roasting tray or pan
3. Roast 20 minutes
4. Stir in the remaining vegetables
5. Roast 10 minutes longer

Alternative cooking method:

1. Heat oil in a large skillet.
2. Sauté onion until softened, 3-4 minutes.
3. Add garlic and sauté 2 minutes more.
4. Add the sliced squash and sauté for 5 minutes until softened.
5. Stir in the green onions, corn, and green chili and sauté for 3 more minutes.
6. Stir in the tomato. Remove from heat.
7. Season with salt and pepper, and then divide into 6 equal portions to serve.

Vegetables should be tender but not mushy or crunchy.

Winter Options:

In winter, instead of zucchini and yellow squash; use butternut, or acorn squash. Peel and cube the squash and use it to replace the summer squash. Frozen corn kernels can be used instead of fresh corn.

Nutrition Facts

Nutrient name	Nutrient value	Unit
Calories	140	—
Total fat	8	g
Saturated fat	1	g
Trans fat	0	g
Cholesterol	0	mg
Sodium	110	mg
Carbohydrate	16	g
Dietary fiber	3	g
Sugars	3	g
Protein	3	g
Vitamin A	—	IU
Vitamin C	—	mg
Calcium	—	mg
Iron	—	mg

This dish qualifies for USDA low calories, low saturated fat, low sodium, and cholesterol free.

Recipe: Turkey Tacos

Serves 6

Ingredients

- ½ pound ground turkey
- 1 Tbsp olive oil
- ½ onion, diced
- 1 garlic clove
- 1 8oz can tomato sauce
- 1 tsp ground cumin
- 1 tsp chili powder
- ¾ cup shredded Monterey jack or cheddar cheese
- 2 Tbsp chopped cilantro
- Salt and pepper to taste (1/4 tsp to start)
- 6 whole wheat tortillas – fajita size (30 g each) or try corn tortillas

Directions

1. Heat a large non-stick pan over medium heat
2. Add olive oil and onion.
3. Sauté onion until translucent, 3-4 minutes
4. Add ground turkey and sauté until browned (3-5 minutes)
5. Add garlic and sauté 1 minute more
6. Add tomato sauce, cumin, chili powder, salt and pepper.
7. Simmer 10 minutes.
8. Layer tortillas on a baking sheet and cover with aluminum foil place in oven for 10 minutes while meat is simmering.
9. Spoon approximately 1/3 cup meat mixture per tortillas.
10. Garnish with 2 Tbsp cheese and cilantro

Nutritional Values

Nutrient Name	Nutrient Value	Unit
Calories	320	
Total Fat	18	g
Saturated Fat	7	g
Trans Fat	0	g
Cholesterol	65	mg
Sodium	540	mg
Carbohydrates	17	g
Dietary Fiber	9	g
Sugars	2	g
Protein	21	g
Vitamin A		IU
Vitamin C		mg
Calcium		mg
Iron		mg

Fresh Fruit

Serves 4

Ingredients

- ¼ pound fruit per person

Directions

1. Rinse, dry, and slice fruit onto a platter for serving.

Sample fruit combinations:

- Assorted berries like strawberries, blueberries, raspberries, and blackberries.

- Melon, like cantaloupe, and honeydew

- Exotic fruit, like mango, pineapple, and bananas

- Stone fruit, like plums, nectarines, peaches, and apricots.

- Fall fruit, like apples and pears.

- Winter fruit, like oranges, nectarines, and kiwi.

Nutrition varies by type of fruit

Appendix A: Glossary of Terms

These are some common terms you may run across in recipes. Many are used in the class recipes.

Kitchen Primer Dinner's Ready —participant handout

Baking
A general term meaning to cook food in the oven. There are several different ways to cook food in the oven. Dry hot heat over 400°F is typically called **roasting.** A lower temperature of 350°F is usually referred to as baking.

Blanching
A general term means cooking the ingredient just to soften the food a bit for easier processing or eating. It might be used for cured meats (salt pork) to reduce the saltiness. Often vegetables or fruit are blanched in order to allow the skin to be peeled before processing further. The basic technique is to bring a pot of water to boil and then place the ingredient into the boiling water for a short amount of time. The amount of time varies by ingredient. Sometimes blanching is also called **parboiling**.

Brown
Browning is a cooking technique that allows a meat or vegetable to become seared quickly over medium high heat. Usually it gets brown marks from the heat of the pan. Typically, after browning, liquid is added to the pan to bring up flavors from the bits attached to the pan. The ingredient is then simmered slowly to finish cooking.

Chop
Cutting into rough pieces. You can chop coarsely (into big pieces) or finely (into small pieces).

Dice
To cut food into tiny (about 1/8- to 1/4-inch) cubes.

Grill
A method of quickly searing meat over a barbeque or in a special pan to give the meat brown marks.

Ice bath
An ice bath is a quick way to cool off a pot that has been on the stove for a while. It is used prior to placing the pot into the refrigerator. Placing a hot pot into a refrigerator may bring the temperature of all stored items too high. Cool by plunging the pot into a pan or sink full of water and ice so that the pot is covered half way up. Stir the contents of the pot to cool it down; be careful that the water is not too high up the side of pot because you don't want water to get into cooked ingredients.

Julienne
Foods that have been cut into very thin, matchstick strips. The food is first cut into 1/8-inch-thick slices. The slices are stacked, and then cut into 1/8-inch-thick strips. The strips may then be cut into whatever length is desired.

Mince
To cut into very small pieces, smaller than chopped

Pickle Pickling is a way to prepare vegetables soaked in an acidic liquid, like vinegar or lemon juice. The acid in the liquid softens the vegetable over a period of time. Vegetables can be pickled by letting them marinade without heat. However, in the case of "pickles" the vegetable is processed with heat in jars in a special way so that the vegetable is preserved for a long period of time, up to 1 year or longer. Cucumbers, carrots, onions, and radishes are common vegetables that are pickled.

Poach Poaching is a method of cooking an ingredient, such as meat or vegetables by slowly simmering in warm liquid with herbs and spices until cooked. Typical poaching liquids are broth, wine or water.

Roasting Dry hot heat over 400°F is typically called **roasting.**

Roux Roux is a mixture of equal parts flour and butter or other fat that is slowly stirred in a pan over low heat until it is lightly toasted. It is used to thicken sauces and soups.

Sauté Sautéing is a cooking technique in which food is cooked quickly in a small amount of oil or other fat in a skillet or sauté pan over direct heat.

Sear A method of cooking quickly over high heat to seal in juices and flavor of an ingredient. It is typically used as a technique for meat and poultry.

Soft-ball stage Soft ball stage is a reference for candy-making and jam. It refers to the point when the sugar is melted and combined with other ingredients and then starts to thicken. When the mixture reaches a temperature 238-240°F the melted sugar should be able to form a small ball. Test by dropping a bit of melted sugar mixture into a glass of ice water, it should cling together and when removed from the water, it can be rolled into a tiny ball.

Trinity Onions, green pepper and celery are called the *trinity* and are the basis for almost every Creole and Cajun recipe.

Appendix B: Check what you learned

For your convenience, a comprehensive quiz for the week is provided. You may wish to use this "Check what you've learned" for tracking purposes.

Dinner's Ready: Check what you've learned

NAME_____   DATE_____

Questions:

True/False – respond true or false to the following questions:

1. When passing a knife to another person; always present the blade or tip to them.

2. There are 8 common food allergies that we reviewed this week.

3. Always make sure a knife is clean and dry before using it.

4. It's a good idea to use the blade to scrape food off of a cutting board.

5. It's best to leave a soiled knife in warm soapy water while you prepare the rest of your meal.

6. Always use a cutting board to protect your counter or table top.

7. If a knife falls it's best to try to catch it before it hits the ground.

8. Dice and chop are sometimes used interchangeably in recipes.

9. Refrigerate or freeze perishables, prepared food, and leftovers within two hours.

10. It is important to cook meats, fish, and poultry correctly to ensure that all bacteria are killed.

11. It's a good idea to read food labels; especially if you have food allergies.

Multiple choice – select the best answer from a to c

1. A good way to store a knife is:
   a. Laying flat in a drawer with a knife guard
   b. In a knife block
   c. Both a. & b. are good ways to store knives.

2. Always keep your knife sharp. The following helps to keep the knife sharp.
   a. Never scrape food off a cutting board with the blade.
   b. Never use a knife for anything except for cutting.
   c. All of the above.

3. It is important in food safety to
   a. Plan, Find, Gather, Cook, Serve,
   b. Clean, Separate, Cook, and Chill

4. Which of the following are common food allergens?
   a. Soy
   b. Milk
   c. Peanuts.
   d. All of the above

Fill in the blank for the following questions:

1. Dry heat over 400°F is typically called _____

2. _____ refers to food cut into tiny (about 1/8- to 1/4-inch) cubes.

3. USDA recommends you make _____ of your plate fruits and vegetables.

4. _____ is a method of cooking that allows a meat or vegetable to become seared quickly over medium heat.

5. _____refers to foods that have been cut into very thin, matchstick strips

6. Can you name the four meals typically eaten throughout the day?

a._____

b._____

c._____

d._____

7. If you are a 10-year-old boy or girl, MyPlate recommends you eat 2½ cups of vegetables a day. When would you eat your vegetables?

_____

8. What are three types of food you need on a healthy plate?

a._____

b._____

c._____

9. According to USDA how much of your grains should be whole grains?

_____

10. What type of grains can be part of a healthy plate?

_____

11. What are two ways you can reduce the amount of fat you eat?

a._____

b._____

12. Name three high protein foods that would fit on a healthy plate?

    a._____

    b._____

    c._____

12. Which of the following are common food allergies?
    a. eggs
    b. fruit
    c. milk

13. Casein is another name for:

    a. wheat
    b. milk
    c. fish
    d. soy

14. If you have a food allergy, you should read food labels.

    True or False

15. Almonds are a type of ____ that many people are allergic to.

    a. tree nut
    b. soy
    c. fish

Appendix C: Optional Desserts

Recipe: Basic Fruit Brown Betty – use any season

Serves 12

Ingredients

- 4-5 cups sliced fruit (1 ½ pounds) (see suggestions below by season)
- ¼ cup coconut oil or unsalted butter + 2 Tbsp
- ¼ cup fresh lemon juice
- 2 Tbsp brown sugar
- 1 cup dates pitted and chopped - optional
- 1 ¼ cup whole wheat flour
- 1 ½ cup old fashioned or quick-cooking oatmeal
- 1 tsp ground cinnamon
- ½ tsp salt
- ¼ cup water

Directions

1. Preheat oven 350°
2. Use 2 Tbsp of coconut oil or butter to grease inside 13- x 9-inch inch heatproof glass baking dish
3. Rinse, , drain, and slice fruit
4. Place fruit in baking dish
5. Pour lemon juice over fruit and toss gently
6. Melt butter in a medium bowl in microwave for 30-60 seconds. (Alternatively, melt in a medium pot on top of the stove.)
7. Add brown sugar, flour, oatmeal, cinnamon and salt to the melted butter. Mixture should be crumbly and resemble coarse pebbles.
8. Crumble topping evenly over fruit
9. Place in oven and bake for 50-60 minutes, until the fruit is tender, and the topping is golden brown.
10. Serve warm with vanilla ice cream or crème fraiche. (optional)

Nutritional Values

Nutrient Name	Nutrient Value	Unit
Calories	160	
Total Fat	6	g
Saturated Fat	4	g
Trans Fat	0	g
Cholesterol	0	mg
Sodium	100	mg
Carbohydrates	22	g
Dietary Fiber	4	g
Sugars	0	g
Protein	5	g
Vitamin A		IU
Vitamin C		mg
Calcium		mg
Iron		mg

This dish qualifies for USDA cholesterol-free using coconut oil

Nutrition varies with fruit added.

Summer Fruit
Nectarines, plums, peaches are great choices
Fall
Apples or pears
Winter
Use frozen fruit such as berries, peaches, or other fruit. Apples are also often available in winter.
Spring
Berries are wonderful in the spring and early summer, raspberries and also rhubarb is good.
Note: Rhubarb, plums, or other tart fruit may require extra sugar.

Recipe: Cannon Banana Surprise – use in winter or spring

This recipe was created during our class at Cannon AFB March 2012.

Ingredients

Serves 4

- 5 Bananas
- 1 Tbsp Brown Sugar

Directions

1. Preheat oven to 400. Line a 13- x 9-inch baking sheet with parchment paper or aluminum foil.
2. Peel bananas
3. Cut banana's in half, crosswise
4. Cut banana halves in half again
5. tt Arrange banana pieces on the prepared baking sheet
6. Sprinkle brown sugar on bananas
7. Pat brown sugar down if needed to cling to the bananas.
8. Bake for 10 minutes, or until the bananas are heated through and the topping is crunchy.

Nutritional Values

Nutrient Name	Nutrient Value	Unit
Calories	140	
Total Fat	0	g
Saturated Fat	0	g
Trans Fat	0	g
Cholesterol	0	mg
Sodium	0	mg
Carbohydrates	37	g
Dietary Fiber	4	g
Sugars	21	g
Protein	2	g
Vitamin A		IU
Vitamin C		mg
Calcium		mg
Iron		mg

This dish qualifies for USDA low calories, low fat, and saturated fat-free, cholesterol-free, sodium free

Recipe: Banana Freeze – use in summer

This recipe was created during our class at Tinker AFB July 2012.

Ingredients

Serves 4

- 5 Bananas
- 1 cup strawberries or mixed fresh seasonal berries
- 2 Tbs. unsweetened cocoa powder or semi-sweet chocolate chips, optional
-

Directions

1. Cut bananas into slices – place in the freezer in a zip lock bag for 1-2 hours.
2. Place berries in a saucepan over medium-high heat.
3. Cook berries for about 10 minutes to make a sauce., Set aside until ready to serve
4. Remove bananas from freezer and puree in a food processor or blender.
5. Place a scoop of frozen banana puree in individual bowls
6. Top each scoop with 2 Tbsp of the reserved berry sauce
7. If cocoa or chocolate chips are available, sprinkle on top.

Nutritional Values

Nutrient Name	Nutrient Value	Unit
Calories	150	
Total Fat	1	g
Saturated Fat	0	g
Trans Fat	0	g
Cholesterol	0	mg
Sodium	0	mg
Carbohydrates	38	g
Dietary Fiber	5	g
Sugars	20	g
Protein	2	g
Vitamin A		IU
Vitamin C		mg
Calcium		mg
Iron		mg

This dish qualifies for USDA low calories, low fat, and saturated fat-free, cholesterol-free, sodium free

Recipe Very Berry Cobbler – use in winter

Serves 12

This recipe was created during our class at Cannon AFB March 2012.

Ingredients

- 1 ½ sticks (3/4 cup) unsalted butter
- 1 1/2 cups dried mixed fruit (such as prunes, apricots, and pear) or 6 oz. dried blueberries
- 1 1/2 cups raisins or 6 oz. sweetened dried cranberries
- 1 1/2 cups pitted and sliced dates (about 6 oz)
- Juice of 1 orange (1/4 cup)
- 1/4 cup brown sugar
- 1 cup (whole wheat) flour
- 3/4 cup old fashioned or quick-cooking rolled oats
- 1 1/2 tsp vanilla extract, optional
- 1 tsp. Ground cinnamon

Directions

1. Preheat oven to 350
2. Grease a13- x 9- inch baking dish with 1 Tbsp butter
3. Mix dry fruit in bowl
4. Squeeze orange juice over the fruit
5. Combine remaining butter, flour, oats, vanilla (if using) and cinnamon in a separate bowl, set aside
6. Spread fruit mixture in the prepared baking dish
7. Crumble oat mixture over top of fruit
8. Place i for 20 minutes, until the fruit is tender, and the topping is golden

Nutritional Values

Nutrient Name	Nutrient Value	Unit
Calories	230	
Total Fat	5	g
Saturated Fat	2.5	g
Trans Fat	0	g
Cholesterol	10	mg
Sodium	5	mg
Carbohydrates	45	g
Dietary Fiber	5	g
Sugars	18	g
Protein	4	g
Vitamin A		IU
Vitamin C		mg
Calcium		mg
Iron		mg

This dish qualifies for USDA low sodium, low cholesterol

Notes

Made in the USA
Columbia, SC
12 July 2022

63310428R00050